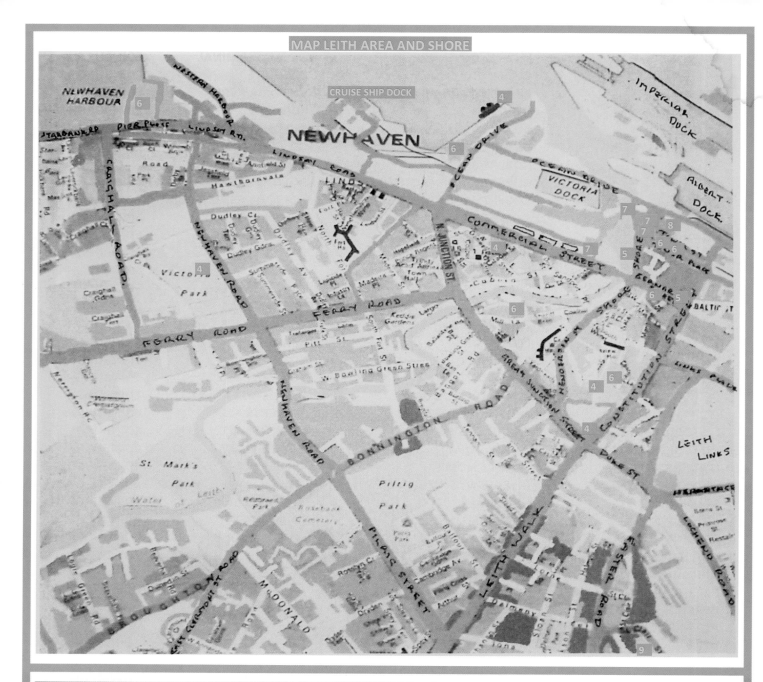

CRINGLETIE HOUSE
A Luxury Castle Hotel near Peebles
JUST 40 MINUTES FROM EDINBURGH
Accommodation • Bar Meals
Restaurant Dining • Afternoon Tea
and Weddings... in fact whatever
the occasion you are always very welcome.

More info @ www.cringletie.com, call 01721 725750 or email enquiries@cringletie.com

QUEEN VICTORIA

KING EDWARD VII

KING EDWARD VII

There is a statue of Queen Victoria's eldest son Edward who became king on her death in Victoria Park, Newhaven Road Edinburgh. King Edward VII was educated at the University of Edinburgh, Oxford University and Cambridge University and went on to marry Alexandra, eldest daughter of King Kristian IX of Denmark.

TRINITY HOUSE MUSEUM

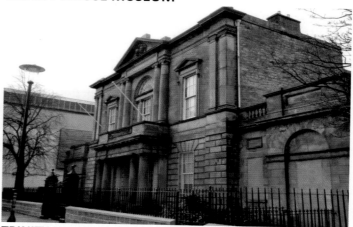

QUEEN VICTORIA Statue Edinburgh
(24 May 1819 – 22 Jan 1901) This Statue was to commemorate the reign of Queen Victoria and her visit to Leith in 1842. She died in 1901. It is also a war memorial to the memory of the Scots Guards from the area that died in the Boar War. It was unveiled by Lord Roseberry who was the Liberal Prime Minister 1894-5 and the ceremony was watched by a crowd of over 20,000 people. Leith became a part of Edinburgh in 1920. The meaning of Leith is broad river.

TRINITY HOUSE MUSEUM EDINBURGH
The original mariner's house built in 1555 on this site was an Almshouse for the retired and poor that wished to stay within the seafaring community. The present building replacing the original Almshouse was built in 1816. Explore Trinity house and see the treasures the mariners returned home with from their travels. There are old marine maps, navigation equipment and ships models. There are also paintings and manuscripts that tell the stories of the sailors of the 14th century to this day.

ROYAL YACHT BRITANNIA is the former Royal Yacht of the British monarch Queen Elizabeth II. The ship is now permanently moored at Ocean Terminal in Edinburgh. The Britannia is the 83rd vessel since the first Royal yacht owned by King Charles II in 1660. It is the second Royal yacht to bear the name Britannia, the first being the famous racing cutter built for the Prince of Wales in 1893. Have a day out and look around the famous Yacht. Now the rich and famous hire the ship for the evening for dinner parties.

THE CITADEL ARCHWAY is the only remains of Leith Citadel built by Oliver Cromwell's troops in 1656. Located next to what was St Ninian's Church. When the Citadel was first built it stood alone next to the beach. Leith was fought over by the English and French and eventually a treaty was signed. The Citadel was a fortification where retreating troops would go when the main walls of the city defences were breached. Leith Citadel was one of the largest as its location to Edinburgh made it an important site to control. The other Citadels that were built were in Perth Inverness, Ayr and (Inverlochy) now Fort William. In 1827 Leith became an independent Parliamentary Burgh which lasted less that 100 years as in 1920 it became a part of Edinburgh. The first recorded mention of Leith was in 1143. Leith was so important that even the American Navy under John Paul Jones tried to capture the port of Leith.

BURNS STATUE IN LEITH

ROBERT BURNS (25 January 1759 – 21 July 1796) Robert Burns died at the age of 37. He was known as the Ploughman poet. He is widely regarded as the national poet of Scotland. Burns was born two miles south of Ayr, in Alloway South Ayrshire, Scotland. Robert Burns was the eldest of seven children. He travelled the world and had many love interests and had 9 children. Robert Burns is buried in St. Michael's Churchyard, Dumfries, Scotland. Robert Burns' brother Gilbert Burns (1760 – 1827) and mother, Agnes Broun 17 March 1732 – 14 January 1820 (and later his sister Annabella) moved to Bolton East Lothian from Ayrshire. Gilbert oversaw the building of the new Bolton parish church which was completed in 1809. The cottage at Grant's Brae is no longer there, the house was demolished and a roadside monument stands in its place. No more than one hundred yards northeast lies the drinking well used by the Burns family. It was lovingly restored in 1932 and dedicated to Agnes Broun. The dedication states:

"Drink of the pure crystals and not only be ye succoured but also refreshed in the mind. To the mortal and immortal memory and in noble tribute to her, who not only gave a son to Scotland but to the whole world and whose own doctrines he preached to humanity that we might learn?

THE WELL pictured below is where Robert Burns mother Agnes Burns (nee Broun) collected the water for the household needs. The house where she lived (Grants Brae) with her son Gilbert and daughter Annabella, brother and sister of Robert Burns is near to Bolton East Lothian. Agnes Burns died 14 January 1820 age 88 years and is buried in Bolton Church yard as are Gilbert, Annabella and Gilbert's daughter.

GRANT'S BRAE BOLTON

THE WORDS FROM THE MONUMENT AT GRANT'S BRAE
NEAR THIS SPOT STOOD THE HOUSE IN WHICH, LIVED AND DIED, THE MOTHER, BROTHER AND SISTER OF SCOTLAND'S NATIONAL POET ROBERT BURNS

BURNS FAMILY WELL

KING'S LANDING The King's Landing is the historic occasion of George the IV becoming the first monarch to stand on Scottish shores since Charles II in 1651. It came about by an invitation from Sir Walter Scott and Henry Dundas, (a very powerful politician at the time). This is when the kilt and tartan wear became popular. The plaques can be seen on the Shore where the Cruz Restaurant is berthed.

GURU NANAK GURDWARA

KING'S LANDING
OPPOSITE THIS SPOT KING GEORGE IV LANDED ON 15th AUGUST 1822. AN HISTORIC VISIT ARRANGED MAINLY BY SIR WALTER SCOTT FOR THE BICENTENARY OF WHOSE BIRTH THIS PLAQUE WAS ERECTED

GURU NANAK GURDWARA EDINBURGH

The first Sikh families to arrive in Edinburgh were in 1958 from the Punjab. The Sikh place of worship is a Gurdwara and the first Gurdwara was a house in Leith in 1964. In 1976 the present Gurdwara was opened at 1 Sheriff Brae Edinburgh. Previous to the Gurdwara it was St Thomas's Church which was built in 1843.
The Sikh religion was founded by Guru Nanak, he was born in 1469 A.D. It is believed that the Sikh religion was first preached in 1496 in the Punjab by Guru Nanak.

NEWHAVEN HARBOUR AND VILLAGE

Newhaven (new harbour) is located on the River Forth and has a small harbour that services a number of local fishing boats. It is now part of Edinburgh but once was a small independent village where the local people lived of the sea, between fishing and ship building. The reason that ship building took place here was due to the depth of the sea. The locals were called Bow tows. The Newhaven area has history as far back as the 1400s and connections with King James III and James IV who had the largest ships of their time built in Newhaven. One of which was the Great Michael, a Man-O-War which was part of the Royal Scottish Navy. Now around the Harbour are a number of restaurants and a hotel on the sea side.

SOUTH LEITH PARISH CHURCH The first mention of Leith in history was when David I gave the lands to the monks of Holyrood in the middle of the 12th century. The first church built was St Mary's in 1483, over the centuries famous people have used the church such as Mary of Guise and Oliver Cromwell. The church has been used as a prison and the General Assembly was held here. Many parts of the church have been replaced since first built, with the ceiling being replace during the renovations of 1847, a Hammer beam ceiling was installed which is still present and will take your breath away.

LEITH BANK was established in 1792 and printed Leith bank notes and was trading from its premises in Bernard Street from 1806. It was common place for towns in Scotland to print their own money. The funding would come from local wealth merchants. Leith Bank did not stay open long as it closed due to lack of funds in 1842.

GOVERNOR JOHN HUNTER

HMS SIRIUS built in Leith was the flagship of the First Fleet, It set out from Portsmouth, England, in 1787 to establish the first European colony in New South Wales, Australia.

SHORE GATES AND CANON

THE GATES TO LEITH stand with two cannon from the 16th century once part of the artillery that protected the Leith Docks from invaders. In the centre a bust of Governor John Hunter, son of a Leith ship master and second in command aboard H.M.S. Sirius when they found the colony of New South Wales in 1788. John Hunter became the Governor of New South Wales from 1795-1800.

CHRISTIAN SALVESEN HARPOON GUN.
Christian Salvesen ran a Whaling company from Leith in the late 1800s. Whale Oil was a very important commodity as it was used for the oil for lamps, machine lubrication, margarine, soap and glycerine for explosives. The gun came from one of the whale catchers run by the Salvesen Company who ran one of the world's largest Whaling fleets, all registered in Leith.

SANDY IRVINE ROBERTSON OBE,
Wine merchant, charity promoter and founder of the Scottish Business Achievements Awards Trust. After his premature death, his friends commissioned a bronze statue which sits on the waterfront at the estuary of the Water of Leith. Behind is a harpoon gun from Port Leith Whaling Station, and the Victoria Swing Bridge that was built in 1874.

COMMERCIAL QUAY LEITH

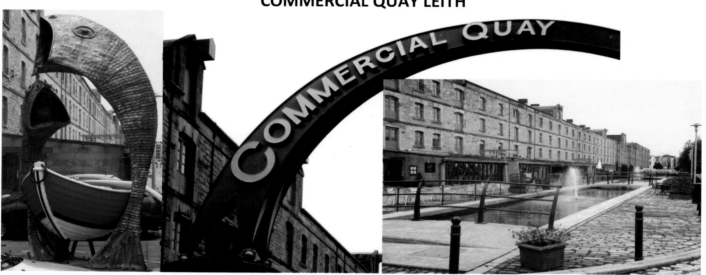

Take a trip to the redeveloped area of the commercial quayside where you will find many types of open air restaurants and just a short stroll away from the Royal Yacht Britannia and the indoor shopping mall Ocean Terminal.

LIGHTHOUSE BEACON The original position of the lighthouse beacon was in Burntisland, Fife (1876) and was moved to its present position in 1990. The roman numerals that can be seen on the front of the lighthouse show the date when it was first used.

VICTORIA SWING BRIDGE 1874
This bridge formerly carried a road, railway crossing and footpaths and was the largest swing bridge in Great Britain. The original Victoria Swing Bridge across the Inner Harbour linked the Albert Dock to the Victoria Dock and was built in 1874. The bridge is now static and is used as a footpath to cross the mouth of the Water of Leith.

SIGNAL TOWER

MALMAISON HOTEL   (SAILOR'S HOME)

THE SIGNAL TOWER built in 1685. The stone tower you can see today was originally higher by at least two further floors. The battlements were built during the Napoleonic war when the tower became the signal tower relaying flag messages to incoming ships.

THE SAILOR'S HOME built in 1883 was accommodation for sailors whose ships were in port. Look for the angel above the door an emblem for the seaman's mission, now a luxury hotel. The Memorial to merchant seamen can be seen in front of the building.

MEMORIAL TO SCOTLAND'S MERCHANT NAVY SEAMEN

The Memorial takes the form of a 5.5 metre sandstone column featuring seafaring scenes in bronze relief. It is possible to see navigators with charts, a ship's cook, stokers, engineers, and seamen hauling lines. The Shore was chosen as the location for this new Memorial because Leith was Scotland's premier port for more than 300 years, and served as Edinburgh's trading port for more than 700 years. In addition, the Memorial recognises the 132 years of service dedicated to the Merchant Navy by Leith Nautical College (1855-1987) and its training ship, "Dolphin" (1944- 1979).

HIBERNIAN FOOTBALL CLUB (EASTER ROAD)

Hibernian was founded by Irish football enthusiasts in 1875 and the name came from the Roman for Ireland (Hibernian). The East Meadows hosted the first Edinburgh Derby with Heart of Midlothian on Christmas day 1875. The present home of Hibernian opened in 1893. In 1955 Hibernian were the first British side to play in European competition. Hibernian won the Scottish Cup in 1902. The Celtic football Club was also formed as a west of Scotland Hibernian but the name was changed as to stop any confusion when playing against each other.

MEADOWBANK SPORTS STADIUM The Stadium was built for the Commonwealth Games in 1970 and was the first venue to hold the Commonwealth games on two occasions. The second games in 1986 were unsuccessful due to the British Governments support of apartheid in South Africa as many countries boycotted the games. There are many varied events held in Meadowbank Stadium throughout the year antiques fares, international competition and local club sports teams still make good use of the stadium. The Stadium was also used for football and the greatest track cyclist of all time, multiple Olympic gold medal winner Sir Chris Hoy started his cycling career here.

COADE PILLARS

The pillars were originally in the garden of Argyle House Hope Lane Portobello. They are constructed from moulded blocks of Coade stone named after Eleanor Coade the inventor of the artificial stone which she called Litho di pyra (which is an ancient Greek word for stone twice fired). Her work can be seen all over the world and is on some of the most prominent buildings in the UK including Buckingham Palace. She died at the age of 98. Coade Stone is no longer used as Portland Cement was invented and the factory ceased trading in 1833. The Pillars can be seen in a garden of Portbello Promanade at the foot of John Street.

THE GREAT LAFAYETTE

Sigmund Neuberger, was born on 25 February 1871 in Munich, Germany and died on 9 May 1911 and is buried in Edinburgh's Piershill Graveyard. He was a famous illusionist and was the highest paid magician of his time. He became one of the highest-paid performers in Vaudeville. The Great Lafayette's affection was his dog Beauty a terrier given to him as a pup by fellow conjurer and admirer Harry Houdini. His dog is also buried in the graveyard.

PIERSHILL GRAVEYARD Opened 1887 with a large Jewish burial section, including a memorial dedicated "to the memory of the Jewish soldiers of Edinburgh who gave their lives in the 1st World War. The cemetery was also the first in Scotland to permit an officially designated animal burial section.

Joppa was a major supplier of salt from the 1600s to 1953 when the last salter closed for business. Salt was extracted from the sea by evaporation on large metal pans heating the salt water which evaporated to leave the salt. The oldest House in the area Rock Cottage which was used by the salt workers. It was originally a lodge owned by a wealth land owner in the 1500s.

ROCK COTTAGE

PORTOBELLO BEACH

Portobello was created as a burgh by Act of Parliament in 1833, and became a part of Edinburgh in 1896.

It is a beach resort located three miles (5 km) to the east of the city centre of Edinburgh, with a promenade that stretches from Seafield on the outskirts of Leith to Joppa just outside Musselburgh. Portobello was at its peak as a resort in the late 19th century. Now Portobello Sailing and Rowing Club use the area for sailing kayaking and surfing. On the good summer days the beach is crowded with sun lovers and people out for a stroll along the promenade. Portobello grew from a small coastal village called Figgate where smugglers and highwaymen would hideout. The name Portobello has been recorded in manuscripts as far back as 1739.

POTTERY KILNS

PORTOBELLO POTTERIES A pottery factory has stood near the Figgate Burn in Portobello since 1770. These are the only surviving kilns of their kind in Scotland from a once thriving industry that goes back over 200 years. The pottery closed in 1972 and moved to a new factory in Crieff Perthshire.

SIR HARRY LAUDER was born in the cottage 3 Bridge Street Portobello in 1870. Sir Harry Lauder was a world wide musical entertainer and three of his most famous songs were Roamin in the Gloamin, I Love a Lassie and Keep right on to the end of the road. Sir Harry Lauder was the highest paid entertainer of his time and the first UK artist to sell one million records.

THE TOWER at Portobello was built in 1785 by Mr James Cunningham from stones window sills and lintels from properties that were knocked down to allow the South Bridge in Edinburgh to be built.

SIR HARRY LAUDER'S BIRTH PLACE

WILLIAM (NED) BARNIE ENGLISH CHANNEL SWIMMER SCIENCE TEACHER 1898 - 1983

William Barnie known as Ned was the first Scotsman to swim the English Channel. At the age of 54 Ned was also the oldest person to swim the English Channel a record he held for 28 years. He was also the first to swim the English Channel in both directions (on the 28 July 1951 from England to France and on the 16 August 1951 from France to England) within the same year. The house where he lived has a plaque in his honour and can be found in Straiton Place, Portobello.

THE GIRAFFES AT THE OMNI CENTRE

THE TWO GIRAFFES The Giraffes are made of scrap metal from motorbikes and cars and stand proudly outside the Omni Centre. The giraffe's official title is "Dreaming Spires" but they have been nicknamed Martha and Gilbert.

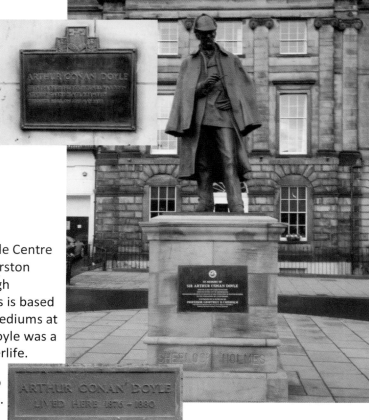

The Sir Arthur Conan Doyle Centre can be found at 25 Palmerston Place where The Edinburgh Association of Spiritualists is based and where you can see mediums at work. Sir Arthur Conan Doyle was a strong believer in the afterlife.

Arthur Conan Doyle's also lived at 23 George Square.

SIR ARTHUR CONAN DOYLE. Sir Arthur Ignatius Conan Doyle was born on 22 May 1859, 11 Picardy Place Edinburgh. The statue stands where his house used to stand Conan Doyle was a novelist, short story writer, poet and doctor of medicine. He is most famous for the stories about the detective Sherlock Holmes. Sir Arthur Conan Doyle was deeply involved in Spiritualism and the Occult. He declared early on in his life that he believed in life after death and the communication with those who passed away. He died in 1930. His last words were addressed to his wife. He whispered "You are wonderful."

The Icelandic national anthem was composed and written in 1874 at 15 London Street Edinburgh.

ST MARY'S CATHEDRAL BROUGHTON STREET EDINBURGH

St Mary's Edinburgh is the cathedral church of the archdiocese of St Andrew and Edinburgh and the first masses were held in August 1814. The Cathedral is the setting for the solemn mass for the opening of the Edinburgh Festival. In 1982 Pope John Paul II visited the Cathedral and prayed at the shrine of Saint Andrew which can be seen within the church building.

WILLIAM HENRY MILLER was born in Craigentinny, an area between Edinburgh and Portobello in 1789. He became a Member of Parliament at the age of 40 for Newcastle-under-Lyme. William Miller was a book collector and opened a library in Britwell Court, near Burnham, Buckinghamshire. The library was said to be one of the most important private collections in Britain. The library and collection, on his death was passed down through the family until 1919, at that time there were no family members left and the collection was broken up and sold. On his death he made a provision in his will to have a mausoleum built on the family estate in Craigentinny Edinburgh. The mausoleum is the the most impressive I have seen and stands over 50 feet (30 meters) in height and goes under ground 40 feet as he had a fear that grave robbers would steal his body. The Mausoleum is decorated with two bas-reliefs based on a Roman Mausoleum. The William Henry Miller Mausoleum was completed in 1856 and stood in a meadow with no other buildings nearby. It stood just near to the Portobello Road on the way to Edinburgh. He left instruction for the bas-reliefs to depict the Overthrow of Pharaoh in the Red Sea and The Song of Moses and Miriam. These were completed and attached to the mausoleum in 1868 and became known as the Craigentinny Marbles. Also within the mausoleum are his parents William Miller and Martha Rawson or Miller, Sarah Marsh and Ellen Marsh all of Craigentinny and Britwell Buckinghamshire.

'THE SONG OF MOSES AND MIRIAM'

THE OVERTHROW OF PHARAOH IN THE RED SEA

MEMORIAL PLAQUE

THE MONUMENT WAS ERECTED TO THE MEMORY OF
WILLIAM HENRY MILLER
AND HIS PARENTS
WILLIAM MILLER AND MARTHA RAWSON OR MILLER
HERE ARE INTERRED
MARTHA MILLER
DIED 11th JANUARY 1827
WILLIAM HENRY MILLER
MP FOR NEWCASTLE-UNDER-LYME
BORN 13th FEBRUARY 1789 DIED 31st OCTOBER 1848
SARAH MARSH
BORN 20th APRIL 1832 DIED AUGUST 6th AUGUST 1880
ELLEN MARSH
BORN 29th AUGUST 1801 DIED 4th NOVEMDER 1861
ALL OF CRAIGENTINNY AND BRITWELL
BUCKINGHAMSHIRE
THE SITE WAS CONSECRATED ON 13th SEPTEMBER 1860
THE SCULPTURES WERE ADDED IN 1868

ARCHITECT	SCULPTOR
DAVID RHIND	ALFRED GATLEY
EDINBURGH	ROME

CRAMOND, CAMMO AND SOUTH QUEENSFERRY

BRIDGE	FORTH RAIL BRIDGE	SOUTH QUEENSFERRY	EDINBURGH	1
BRIDGE	FORTH ROAD BRIDGE	SOUTH QUEENSFERRY	EDINBURGH	1
TOLBOOTH	HIGH STREET	SOUTH QUEENSFERRY	EDINBURGH	1
ROSEBERY FOUNTAIN	HIGH STREET	SOUTH QUEENSFERRY	EDINBURGH	1
PLEWLANDS HOUSE	HOPETOUN ROAD	SOUTH QUEENSFERRY	EDINBURGH	1
DOOR LINTEL	HOPETOUN ROAD	SOUTH QUEENSFERRY	EDINBURGH	1
GLENFORTH DISTILLERY	GOTE LANE	SOUTH QUEENSFERRY	EDINBURGH	1
BLACK CASTLE	HIGH STREET	SOUTH QUEENSFERRY	EDINBURGH	1
PRIORY CHURCH OF ST MARY	HOPETOUN ROAD	SOUTH QUEENSFERRY	EDINBURGH	1
RESTAURANT	HAWES INN	SOUTH QUEENSFERRY	EDINBURGH	1
DROP OFF AND BOARDING	HAWES PIER	SOUTH QUEENSFERRY	EDINBURGH	1
MEMORIAL STONE	HAWES PIER	SOUTH QUEENSFERRY	EDINBURGH	1
MUSEUM	HIGH STREET	SOUTH QUEENSFERRY	EDINBURGH	1
HISTORIC HOUSE	HOPETOUN HOUSE	SOUTH QUEENSFERRY	EDINBURGH	1
ISLAND	INCHGARVIE ISLAND	SOUTH QUEENSFERRY	EDINBURGH	1
BURRY MAN	MUSEUM	SOUTH QUEENSFERRY	EDINBURGH	1
LOONEY DOOK	BEACH	SOUTH QUEENSFERRY	EDINBURGH	1
BUILDING	RNLI	SOUTH QUEENSFERRY	EDINBURGH	1
BUILDING	LAURISTON CASTLE	LAURISTON FARM ROAD	EDINBURGH	1
BUILDING	CAMMO TOWER	CAMMO ROAD	EDINBURGH	1
BUILDING	CAMMO HOUSE	CAMMO ROAD	EDINBURGH	1
BUILDING	CAMMO PIGGERY	CAMMO ROAD	EDINBURGH	1
GARDENS	COMMO HILL	CAMMO ROAD	EDINBURGH	1
NATURE RESERVE	CAMMO HILL	CAMMO ROAD	EDINBURGH	1
SCULPTURE	FISH ON BEACH	CRAMOND VILLAGE	EDINBURGH	2
CHURCH	CRAMOND KIRK	CRAMOND VILLAGE	EDINBURGH	2
ISLAND	CRAMOND ISLAND	CRAMOND VILLAGE	EDINBURGH	2
BUILDING	ROMAN BATH	CRAMOND VILLAGE	EDINBURGH	2
EXCUVATIONS	ROMAN FORT	CRAMOND VILLAGE	EDINBURGH	2
VILLAGE	CRAMOND SHORE	CRAMOND VILLAGE	EDINBURGH	2

The Figgate Burn is where the original name of the area Figgate, now known as Portobello got its name. The park has a pond with a walkway over part of it and it is a great way to see the wild life that is in the park. There are also carvings that can be found. A place for a day out, with plenty of space for the children and with picnic tables provided, bring your lunch and have a picnic.

FIGGATE PARK & GARDENS PORTOBELLO

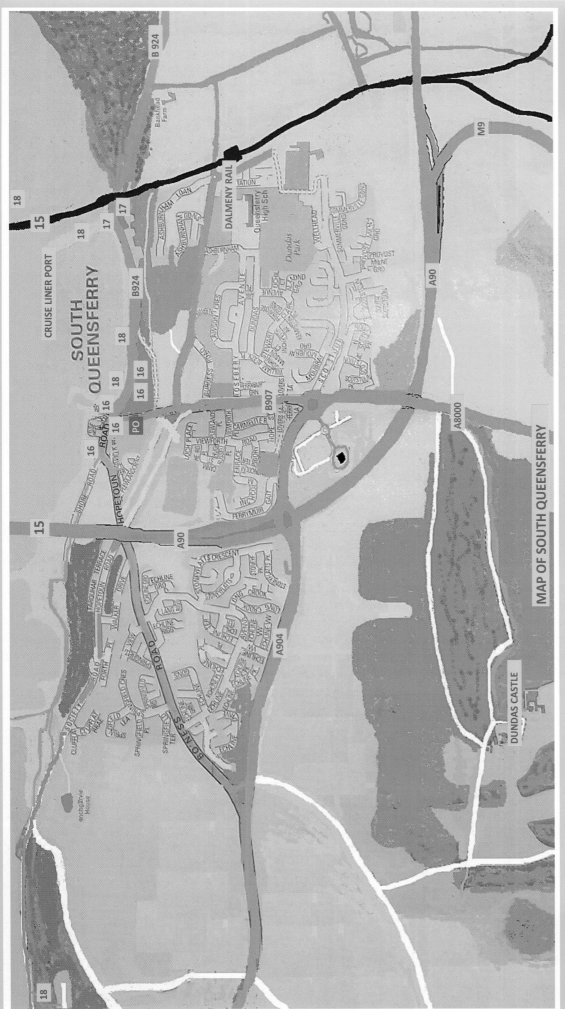

SOUTH QUEENSFERRY

CRUISE LINER PORT

MAP OF SOUTH QUEENSFERRY

There is even more to see in and around Edinburgh the Lothians and Borders. To make it easier for you, you can find out on three web sites which will give you all you need to know Restaurants, accommodation, from the 5 star hotel to the friendly family run guest house or apartments for self- catering, activities, tours, car hire, bars, night clubs, all sports clubs and stadia, libraries, schools and universities, golf courses, museums, consulates, airlines, public transport, taxis, wedding venues and all the things you will need when getting married plus much more.......

One place for everything and everything in one place.

www.allaboutedinburgh.co.uk   www.lothianandborders.com   www.lothianandborders.co.uk

14

THE FORTH RAIL BRIDGE 1890

The Forth Rail Bridge is a cantilever railway bridge over the Firth of Forth. It was opened on 4 March 1890. For over seventy years the Forth Bridge was the only connection across the Firth of Forth without a boat. "Painting the Forth Bridge" is a local expression for a never-ending task, as soon as the painting of the bridge was finished the work would have to start again. The Forth Rail Bridge is the oldest steel constructed cantilever railway bridge in the world. The bridge was designed by Benjamin Baker who was knighted for the work he carried out on the Forth Rail Bridge. He also was involved with the construction of the Aswan Dam.

THE FORTH ROAD BRIDGE 1964

The first plans for a road crossing were made in the 1740s and were finally completed over 200 years later.
The Forth Road Bridge was opened in 04 / 09/ 1964.
The Forth Road Bridge is a suspension bridge that spans the Firth of Forth from the Lothians to Fife.
The bridge replaced the old ferry service that was the only way to cross the river without having to travel up to the only other crossing at Kincardine.
The bridge was designed by Mott, Hay and Anderson and Freeman Fox and Partners.

This point on the River Forth was first known as a crossing in the 11th century by Queen Margaret, as she made frequent trips to Dunfermline and St Andrew. She founded a ferry service to help transport religious pilgrims across the river. The crossing was so well used that small communities emerged on the south and north banks of the river, the ports were both called Queensferry and later changed to South Queensferry and North Queensferry as they are today. The ferry service was used as a passenger ferry for over eight hundred years. The latest bridge is the Queensferry Crossing not yet completed pictured below still under construction (01 / 11 / 2015). The Queensferry Crossing will be the longest three-tower, cable-stayed bridge in the world.

QUEENSFERRY CROSSING UNDER CONSTRUCTION NOVEMBER 2015

THE TOLLBOOTH, SOUTH QUEENSFERRY is located on the High Street, as in all other burgh towns of Scotland the main building was the Tolbooth (jail). The Tolbooth would have been in place around 1630 with the present clock-tower built in 1720. There are two bells in the tower dated 1694 and 1723. The bell dated 1694 was donated by the seamen of South Queensferry. St Marys Church is the oldest recorded building in Queensferry dating from 1441.

ROSEBERY FOUNTAIN

The wall fountain shows the coat of arms of Queensferry a cross and birds. With the arms of Rosebery a half-length Lion rampant holding a Rose dated 1817.

PLEWLANDS HOUSE was built in 1641 for Samual Wilson on his marriage to Anna Ponton. The stone engraving above the door translates to "Christ is my hope" and the letters below are the initials of the betrothed with their marriage date **S.W.** Samuel Wilson **AP** Anna Ponton **1641.** This was a tradition when moving into your family home, a marriage stone would be inscribed on the wall of their house for all to see. There is an example on the wall in Ramsay Lane Edinburgh up from the New Library.

GLENFORTH DISTILLERY SOUTH QUEENSFERRY 1828 South Queensferry has been linked with whisky distilling for Over 170 years the first distillery was built in 1828 near the harbour, to allow the ships to load and unload their cargo without a further journey to the distillery by road. Another famous name from South Queensferry is VAT 69 first bottled in 1882 by William Sanderson and Sons Leith.

THE BLACK CASTLE on the High Street built in 1626 is the oldest surviving house in South Queensferry. When the original owner William Lawrie a sea-captain was lost at sea with his ship and crew, his house maid was accused of paying a beggar-woman to cast a spell to sink the ship, both were tried as witches and found guilty and were burnt at the stake. The Black Castle was also where in the 18th century smugglers would bring in through tunnels from the shore, barrels of contraband brandy.

PRIORY CHURCH OF ST MARY St Mary's was originally the Carmelite Friary. The Carmelites were invited to Queensferry by George Dundas of Dundas in 1330. Dundas Castle stands just outside South Queensferry, presently a private residence.

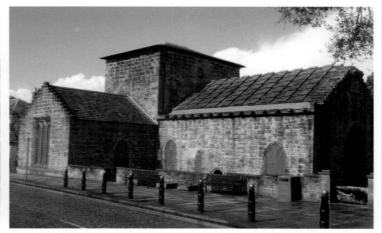

NAMING OF QUEENSFERRY, Queen Margaret encouraged the making of pilgrimages to St Andrews from Edinburgh, which incurred a crossing of the Firth of Forth estuary by boat. Over time Queen Margaret had housing erected on both shores of the Forth which divides Lothian from Fife. This allowed the poor people and pilgrims' shelter and rest after their long journey. She also provided ships to enable the crossing in both directions for no charge.
The settlements grew and were known as Queensferry later to be named North and South Queensferry as they are named today.

THE HAWES INN dates back from the 17th century and stands across from Hawes Pier and the Rail Bridge in South Queensferry. It features in Robert Louis Stevenson's novel Kidnapped during the Jacobite uprisings. **HAWES PIER** is directly under the Forth Rail Bridge and is the point for boats to pick up and drop off passengers from the cruise ships and the boarding point for the Island tours. RNLI has its base here to cover the Forth Estuary.

FORTH BRIDGE MEMORIALS
Thousands of Briggers have worked building, maintaining and restoring the bridge over its 100 plus years of history. A 7 foot high bronze memorial stands at each end of the Rail Bridge in memory of the men who died constructing the bridge, and also to celebrate all that were involved in its completion. The Forth Rail Bridge is the oldest steel constructed bridge of its kind in the world.

SOUTH QUEENSFERRY MUSEUM
This is where the story of the construction of the Forth Bridges can be seen. There are also displays relating to the ferry passage started in the 1100s, fascinating objects and photographs and the history of the town. The Burry Man, Distilleries The Black Castle. All to be seen in the Museum at 53 High Street South Queensferry.

HOPETOUN HOUSE

Lady Margaret Hamilton had the original House built in 1699 for her son Charles Hope who became the 1st Earl of Hopetoun in 1703. Hopetoun House took almost 8 years to complete and became the home of the Hope family from that day to this. In 1721 the house was refurbished and extended to what can be seen today, a magnificent ancestral home. Hopetoun House is well worth a visit for its superb interiors and 6500 acres to explore.

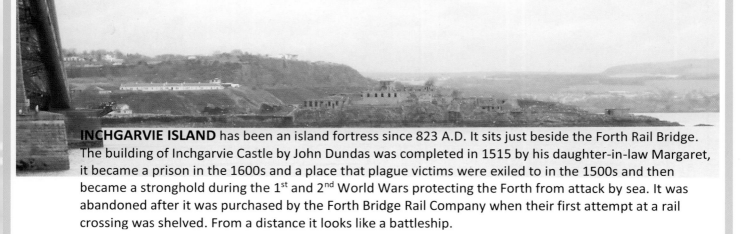

INCHGARVIE ISLAND has been an island fortress since 823 A.D. It sits just beside the Forth Rail Bridge. The building of Inchgarvie Castle by John Dundas was completed in 1515 by his daughter-in-law Margaret, it became a prison in the 1600s and a place that plague victims were exiled to in the 1500s and then became a stronghold during the 1st and 2nd World Wars protecting the Forth from attack by sea. It was abandoned after it was purchased by the Forth Bridge Rail Company when their first attempt at a rail crossing was shelved. From a distance it looks like a battleship.

THE LOONY DOOK

The name is a combination of lunatic and dunk. An event held every year on the first day of the year (January 1st). Any one can join in as all you have to do is dive into the freezing waters of the Firth of Forth on New Year's Day in whatever clothing takes your fancy. Fancy dress, swim wear or a three piece suit, your choice. The event takes place from 9 a.m. on the beach at South Queensferry pictured left.

THE BURRY MAN is a local man covered from head-to-toe in sticky burrs covering his entire body, leaving only the shoes, hands and two eye holes exposed. He walks around the town collecting money for charity. It is a great honour to be picked as the Burry Man as it has been a tradition for over 300 years. The event takes place once a year at the Ferry Fair. Stand face-to-face with the Burry Man in the Queensferry Museum.

THE BURRY MAN

RNLI.

Hawes Pier is also the base for the **R**oyal **N**ational **L**ifeboat **I**nstitution. Founded in 1824 with one aim to save peoples lives at sea.

CAMMO HOUSE, GARDENS, AND NATURE RESERVE

Cammo House was built in the early part of the 1690s by a John Menzies a wealthy businessman and was later sold to Sir John Clerk in 1710. Sir John Clerk with an interest in landscaping set out the gardens of Cammo house over the next several years. The house is now a ruin and the lands are now open to the public. Things to look for are the ruin of Cammo House, the said to be oldest and largest Ash tree in Edinburgh, the East Lodge, Cammo Tower, The Cammo Stane and if very lucky the Ghosts of Cammo House.

CAMMO STANGING STONE

STABLES

RUINS OF CAMMO HOUSE

CAMMO HOUSE RUINS

TREE PLANTED 1854

CAMMO NATURE RESERVE

CAMMO TOWER

CAMMO CANAL

CAMMO WATER TOWER was built in the 1870's and supplied Cammo house with water. The water was run by a pump by a windmill that was on top of the Tower which is no longer there.

LAURISTON CASTLE CRAMOND ROAD SOUTH EDINBURGH

Lauriston Castle is decorated and furnished as it would have been in 1926, when it was bequeathed to the nation by its owner Mrs Reid. Take a walk round the beautiful gardens or meditate in the Japanese garden gifted by Kyoto. The Castle was built at the end of the 16th century for the Napier family. (Alexander Napier was brother of John, inventor and maths genius). Other owners the said to be world's first millionaire John Law 1671-1729.

CRAMOND VILLAGE 8400 B.C. This was the oldest known area of where there is evidence of human settlement in Scotland (8400 B.C.). The Romans used the area as a camp and evidence shows Cramond started to grow as a village in 142 A.D. Cramond was also the first area the residents were called commuters, as the new railway built in 1894 would take the residence of the area to Edinburgh City to work. There are many historic buildings and interesting things to see in Cramond Village a short Taxi ride from Edinburgh city centre. You can also see the Royal Burgess Golf Club the oldest established golf club in the World founded in 1735. The oldest recorded area of human habitation in Scotland is just outside Edinburgh at Howburn dated from (12000 B.C.).

CRAMOND KIRK

ROMAN FORT (BARRACKS)

ROMAN BATH HOUSE SITE

CRAMOND TOWER

SEPTIMIUS SEVERUS was the last Roman Emperor to try and conquer Scotland in 208 AD but died of illness in 210 AD. A previous emperor Antoninus Pius also tried to conquer the Scots but gave up after 30 years about in 140 AD. The Romans failed in their attempts to conquer Scotland and all they left were ruins, walls, roads and bridges which can still be seen today. Both emperors built forts in Cramond about a century apart. This area was inhabited by many hundreds of Romans and was more like a town than a Fort. Don't miss the Cramond Lioness a sandstone sculpture found in 1997 in the river bed at Cramond. Depicting a Lioness devouring a human torso (600b.c – 200b.c.) now in the National Museum in Edinburgh.

THE CRAMOND TOWER once the residence of the Bishop of Dunkeld. Originally built in the 11th century and left vacant for over 300 years it was renovated in the 1970s under strict guidance from historians.

THE BATH HOUSE was found while the car park was being made in 1975. The best preserved Roman Bath House in Scotland. **Cramond Kirk** dates from the 15th century with additions in 1800s. The bell is from Holland as were most church bells in Scotland. **The Stone Fish** Sculpture all of 8 tonnes (8000 Kgs) stands 7 feet high (2.2m) and 10 feet (30.5 m) in length can be found on the beach at Cramond.

CRAMOND ISLAND is accessible by a causeway dependent on tides, have a walk to the island and see the deserted buildings. An Ivy covered Farm house which once was occupied as early as the 1700s and possibly there would have been a Roman lookout tower when Cramond was a Roman strong hold in 200 A.D.

Duddingston Loch with a sanctuary for wild birds. The plaque with the quote by John Thomson one time minister of Duddingston Kirk, 'We're all Jock Tamson's bairns', (Meaning) We are all the same. Duddingston Village full of history and an easy way up Arthur Seat. With steps that take you half way and a gentle slope the remainder of the way to the top. Midpoint a bench for a rest and Dunsapie Loch with a view of East Lothian.

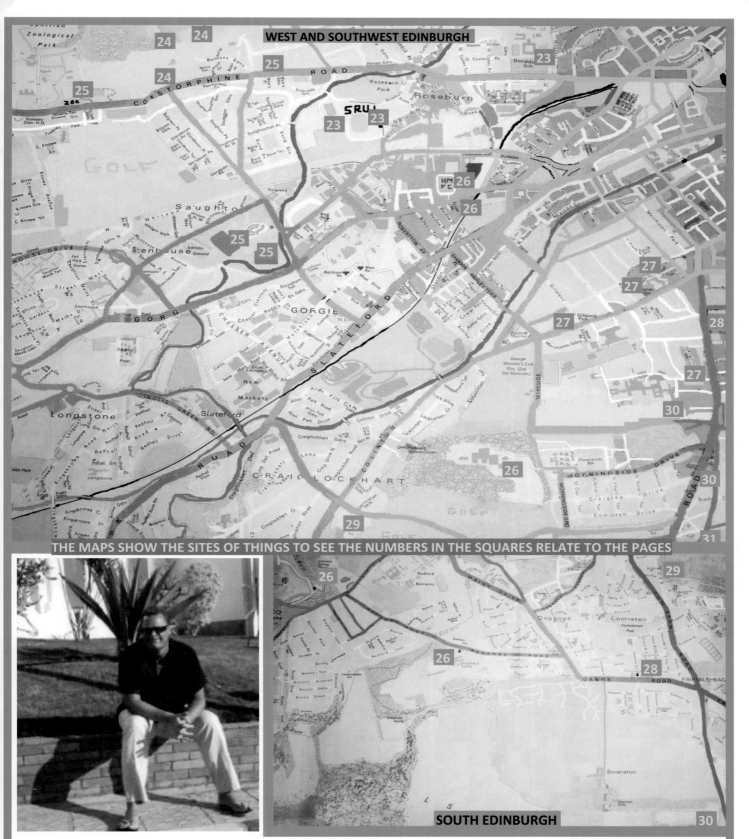

THE MAPS SHOW THE SITES OF THINGS TO SEE THE NUMBERS IN THE SQUARES RELATE TO THE PAGES

SOUTH EDINBURGH

My name is Gary Marshall and I was born and have lived in Edinburgh for over 50 years. All About Edinburgh booklets first came to me when on holiday in Paris France. When my wife and I were looking for the site of the Bastille. We seemed to be going round in circles and finally, finding someone to ask who would speak English, I asked where is the site of the Bastille, the famous Jail from the revelotion? He pointed and said there. We looked into the middle of a roundabout (which we had been round twice) to see a pillar covered in posters, this was the historic site of the jail, The Bastille. I then thought that it must be the same worldwide when visiting places, not knowing what you are actually standing beside or walking past. Over the next 6 years I have put together the 3 All About Edinburgh booklets. It has been a great learning curve and I now know more about my own city than I had in the previous 50 years. I hope you are enjoying this booklet as much as I have when compilling it, and will also enjoy the other two parts of the trilogy.

DONALDSON'S HOSPITAL (SCHOOL) was designed by William Playfair for James Donaldson, a wealth bookseller and printer that lived in Edinburgh in 1830.

James Donaldson on his death left his fortune to build and maintain a building for the deaf and dumb of Edinburgh.

The students in the school were both hearing and non hearing and this lead to the hearing students learning sign language and these students went on to teach sign language around the world. The School moved from Edinburgh to its present location in Linlithgow in 2007.

SCOTTISH RUGBY UNION HEAD QUARTERS MURRAYFIELD STADIUM

The home of Scottish Rugby Union is a 64000 all seated stadium, where Scotland play their home international Rugby matches. Murrayfield Stadium was first opened in 1925 and was renovated in 1994, when it became all seated. Other events that have been held here in the past include the 2000 Rugby league challenge cup final, music concerts such as (The Rolling Stones, Bon Jovi, Madonna, Oasis) and NFL American football. The War memorial Arch and Clock are prominent features of the Stadium's history. Opening from 9 am daily for a free walk around where information boards are present for your help or you can book a guided tour of the stadium.

MURRAYFIELD ICE RINK opened to the public in 1952. It is the largest Rink in Scotland. Events that have been held at the ice rink include Ice Hockey, Figure Skating, Boxing and Basketball. In 1980 a separate curling rink was opened. In 1958, 1963 and 1993 Murrayfield Ice Rink was the venue for The Harlem Globetrotters basketball exhibitions. The ice rink is open to the public and ice skates are available for hire. There is also a curling rink next door. You can also see National League Ice Hockey on a Sunday Evening. (Check with rink for game dates).

Corstorphine Hill

CORSTORPHINE HILL is Edinburgh's largest public park and nature reserve. The hill at 531 feet (161m) is a great place for a day out and ramble, there is a variety of wildlife on Corstorphine Hill including great spotted woodpecker, tawny owl, badger, kestrel, and sparrow hawk.

CORSTORPHINE HILL WALLED GARDEN
The walled garden has been restored by a local volunteer group. They have created a quiet space to sit and relax or read a book.

CORSTORPHINE HILL EDINBURGH At the summit of the Corstorphine Hill is the Clermiston Tower also known as the Scott Tower or the Corstorphine Hill Tower. It is a memorial to Edinburgh's romantic novelist Sir Walter Scott. The tower was built by William Mackie in 1871 on the centenary of Sir Walter Scott's birth. From the parapet at the top the views of the surrounding area are stunning. This was a place Sir Walter Scott would visit and contemplate his scriptures.

ROBERT LOUIS STEVENSON (1850 -1894)

Robert Louis Stevenson was born in Edinburgh on the 13 November 1850 to a wealthy family of Engineers. His grandfather Robert built the Regent Bridge in Waterloo Place Edinburgh to connect the main road to London with Princes Street in the new town bypassing the dirty streets of Leith.

Robert Louis Stevenson never kept good health and spent his summers in North Berwick at the sea side where his Grandfather had a summer residence. The statue pictured is of Thomas Balfour and Alan Breck Stewart departing from Corstorphine Hill Edinburgh. They were the characters in the novel Kidnapped, which was about the Jacobite uprising and the true story of the two main characters. Robert Louis Balfour Stevenson to give his full name was an author of many famous books e.g. Treasure Island, Dr Jekyll and Mr Hyde and Kidnapped.

EDINBURGH ZOO

THE EDINBURGH ZOO (Centenary year 2013) is in the west of Edinburgh, on the main route from the airport. Edinburgh Zoo was opened to the public on 22 July 1913. The Royal Zoological Society of Scotland was founded in 1909 probably best known throughout the world for their Penguins. The Penguins were first brought to Edinburgh by the whaling ships that would call in at Leith. The association with these amazing birds began in January 1903. There are over 180 different animal species in the zoo the most popular are a pair of giant pandas from China.

SAUGHTON PARK, SKATEBOARDING & GLASSHOUSE

Saughton Park at one time had a 9 hole golf course, paddling pool and playing fields. In 1908 the Scottish National Exhibition was held in the park and in 1984 the Winter Garden was opened. In 2010 the largest outdoor skateboard park in Scotland was opened and later a children's play area. There are also football pitches and a sports stadium with a running track. Don't miss the shoe tree where the boarders hang their shoes for luck. In the glasshouse you can see the bust of Ghandi and tropical plants. The gardens are a tranquil place to sit and contemplate. With an award winning Rose Garden, paths, walled gardens and ornamental flowers and not forgetting the glass houses where the winter garden gives the area flowers all year round.

GORGIE CITY FARM opened to the public in 1982 and is open 7 days a week with free entry. The farm animals consist of chickens, ducks, turkeys, goats, pigs and sheep. There is also a cow and a pony. There are pet lodge animals of which rats, rabbits, guinea pigs, hamsters, tortoise and one snake. Come to the only city farm in Edinburgh. Great for children.

HEART OF MIDLOTHIAN FOOTBALL CLUB (GORGIE)

The club was founded in 1874 and played their football in the East Meadows. The East Meadows hosted the first Edinburgh Derby with Hibernian on Christmas day 1875. Main stand opened in 1914 and is still present today.

WILLIAM KINNIMOND BURTON ENGINEER, PHOTOGRAPHER 1856 - 1899

William Kinnimond Burtons family home was Craig House, part of the old Craig house campus of Napier University. In 1877 he was invited by the Meiji Government of Japan to become the first Professor of Sanitary Engineering and lecturer in Rivers, Docks and Harbours at the Imperial University of Tokyo.

He designed new water and drainage systems for Tokyo, (population of one and a half million), and many other towns and cities in Japan and Taiwan. He also designed Japan's first skyscraper, 'Ryounkaku', in Tokyo. William Kinnimond Burton became an icon of modern Japan. He died on 5 August, 1899 at the age of 43.

An impressive tombstone was built in the Aoyama Cemetery in Tokyo.

To this day, people still gather for an annual ceremony to lay flowers on his grave and sing Scottish folk songs. An accomplished photographer he had a book ABC of Modern Photography published in 1882. Burton helped form the Photographic Society of Japan in 1890.

ROBERT LOUIS STEVENSON 1850 – 1894

A statue of Robert Louis Stevenson as a boy sits outside Colinton Parish Church where he attended Sunday worship with his family.

COVENANTERS 1666 The memorial is to remember the covenanters who died at the Battle of Ruillion Green. It was at Colinton where the covenanters turned for home, on their way the Royalist Army lead by Sir Thomas Dalziel caught up with them, just outside Penicuik at Ruillion Green and after a short and bloody battle and many deaths, the Government troops took the Covenanters that survived and imprisoned them in Greyfriar's Covenanters prison where they died, were executed or deported. A few were lucky and escaped.

CLAN NAPIER CREST can be found above the main entrance of The Napier Tower in the Napier University campus in Colinton Road Edinburgh. The clan Coat of Arms are only allowed to be used by the clan chieftain.

THE CLAN CREST IS:
A dexter cubit arm, the hand grasping a Crescent Argent with birds holding the Clan Chiefs coat of arms.
NAPIER FAMILY MOTTO
The meaning of **SANSTACHE** a French word is (**WITHOUT STAIN**).

NAPIER TOWER & NAPIER'S BUST COLINTON ROAD EDINBURGH

JOHN NAPIER a great inventor and Mathematician lived in the Napier Tower that was built by Alexander Napier the second Laird of Merchiston around 1454. John Napier the 8th Laird of Merchiston was born here in 1550. John Napier is best known as the discoverer of logarithms (Napier's bones) in 1614. The bones can be seen in the Scottish National Museum. John Napier also appears to have been the first to intentionally use the frenetic period as a decimal separator in his book Rabdologia published in 1617. Also found in the same book was reference to Napier's bones, numbered rods which were used to perform multiplication and division of any number, also useful in navigation and astronomy. Napier Technical College was opened in 1964 named after John Napier and in 2009 became Edinburgh Napier University. Napier Tower serves as the seat for Clan Napier and stands on the Napier University campus in Colinton Road Edinburgh. The Bust is now on show in the main reception at Colinton. John Napier is buried in St Cuthbert's Graveyard at the west end of Princes Street.

ESTABLISHED 1978

TRADITIONAL CRAFTS,KNITWEAR & TEXTILES ALL MADE IN SCOTLAND

ROYAL MILE
AUTHENTIC SCOTTISH HANDMADE CRAFT AT ITS BEST
164 -166 CANONGATE EDINBURGH
0131 557 2967
CANONGATEJANDC@AOL.COM
WWW.CANONGATECRAFTS.CO.UK

THE CAIY STONE

The Caiy Stane

Standing at over nine feet high on a summit, originally with wide views, this broad slab of red sandstone includes a line of six, probably prehistoric, cup marks on its reverse face.

The stone may have been erected as early as the Neolithic period, possibly before 3000 BC, to denote a ritual or burial place. Records of cairns, cists and urns found in the immediate vicinity show that the hilltop continued to be used for burial in the Bronze Age.

Discovery of these remains led to the supposition that Caiyside Hill was the site of a battle, variously suggested to have involved invading Romans, Danes (Vikings); or Cromwellians. The Caiy Stane, also known as the Kel Stane, the Cat Stane or the Camus Stane, was thought to have been a battle memorial stone.

THE CAIY STANE is located at the side of the walkway on the west side of Caiystane View, a short distance from the junction of Oxgangs Road, Edinburgh. The stone is red sandstone and stands 9 feet 3 inches high (2.75m) with a breadth of 5 foot 9 inches (1.60m). A row of six cup marks can be seen on the back of the prehistoric stone. The stone may have been erected before 3000 BC, as early as the Neolithic period, probably to denote a ritual or burial place. Records of cairns, cists and urns found in the immediate vicinity show that the hilltop continued to be used for burial in the Bronze Age. Discovery of these remains led to the supposition that Caiyside Hill was the site of a battle, suggested to have involved invading Romans, Danes (Vikings) or Cromwellians. The Caiy Stane (Kel Stane), Cat Stane or Camus Stane, was thought to have been a battle memorial stone.

THE BORESTONE The only folklore associated with this site relates to James IV before the battle of Flodden in 1513 when it is alleged that the Royal Standard was pitched in or on the stone when it lay on the Borough Muir nearby. The Bore Stone stands on a pedestal built into the boundary wall of Morningside Parish Church Edinburgh. The surface of the stone displays numerous cup-like markings, none of which are believed to be anything other than natural. After the battle the city wall was built to protect Edinburgh from the English Army.

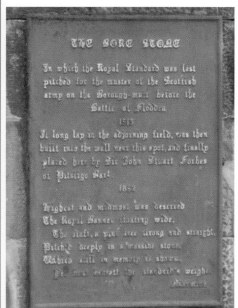

THE BORE STONE

In which the royal standard was last pitched for the muster of the Scottish army on the Borough-Muir before the Battle of Flodden
1513
It long lay in the adjoining field, was then built into the wall near this spot, and finally placed here by Sir John Stuart Forbes of Pitsligo Bart.
1852
Highest and midmost was described
The Royal Banner floating wide.
The staff, a pine tree strong and straight
Pitch'd deeply in a massive stone.
Which still in memory is shown.
Yet bent beneath the standard's weight.
Marmion.

CRAIGLOCKHART CASTLE (TOWER)

All that remains of the Tower a ruin of a 4 floored tower with walls 5 foot thick. It is unknown who built it but the first land owners were the Lockhart's of Lea in the 12th century. However it is thought that the Kincaid family lived there during the reign of James the VI in the late 1500s. The Lochart's or Kincaid's who knows.

LIBERTON TOWER is a 15th century castle with a grand furnished period interior over three floors and also an outside walkway. Built in the 1480s and abandoned in 1610 when the owners moved to a more luxurious house. The Coat of Arms of the first owners can be seen on a carved panel on the south wall.

GILMERTON COVE (CAVES)

The mystery of the Gilmerton Cove a secret hideout for the Knights Templar or an illegal drinking den. It is believed the caves were dug in early 1700s by a local blacksmith as a house. Go down the caves and decide for yourself. They can be found at 16 Drum Street Gilmerton once a village outside Edinburgh.

QUEEN VICTORIA

The wall tablet is to commemorate Queen Victoria's 60 years on the throne in 1897. Look up on the wall just above the shops, up from the Taxi rank in Morningside Road, the plaque is just above a street light.

JESUS CHRIST OF THE LATTER - DAY SAINTS

Arthur's Seat is where the apostle Orsan Pratt of the Church of Jesus Christ of Latter-day Saints when in Edinburgh would climbed to the top of the hill and look down on the city and pray for converts to his church.
Orsan Pratt was one of the leaders of his church and travelled the world recruiting converts and it was in 1840 he recruited in Edinburgh.

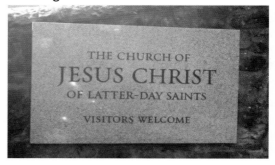

THE BUCK STANE stands at just over 1.00m high by 0.38m at its widest and is 0.28m thick. It stands against a garden wall in a small alcove near the south end of Braid Road. The stone has an information plaque which can be seen on the wall. Tradition associates the Buck Stane with the Barony of Penicuik and the royal hunts on the Borough-Muir. The plaque also says that the stone marks the spot where the buckhounds were let loose when the King of Scotland hunted in the region.

(The wording on the plaque)
This march stone a relic of feudal times occupied a commanding site on the old roman road about 250 yards north from this spot by tradition the name was derived from the stone having marked the place where the buckhounds were unleashed when the king of Scotland hunted in this region.

MOST SUCCESSFUL BRITISH GOLFER THOMAS DICKSON ARMOUR

THOMAS (Tommy) ARMOUR 1896 – 1968 Scotland's most successful golfer was born at 18 Balcarres Street in Morningside and first played golf at the Braid Hills and Bruntsfield Links. Free golf is still available at Bruntsfield Links, where royalty played in the 1400s. Bruntsfield Links was the course where many golf clubs started. The Burghers or now known as The Royal Burgess, the oldest golf club in the world and The Honourable Company of Edinburgh Golfers (Muirfield) where the original 13 rules of golf were first written. At first there were only 5 rules.

Thomas Armour after the First World War moved to the U.S. and as a professional golfer won over 20 professional championships which included The US Open, The PGA Championship, The British Open and was three times Canadian Open champion. Western Golf Club founded in 1899 and based at the Braid Hills golf course which opened in 1889 was where Tommy Armour first joined a golf club in 1912 and his first competition win was in 1913 on the Braids golf course.

BRAIDHILLS GOLF COURSE

18 BALCARRES STREET

THE HANGING OF THOMAS KELLY AND HENRY O'NEIL EDINBURGH

Edinburgh's passion for executing the guilty can be seen in the many places around the Edinburgh streets where executions took place, e.g. The Grassmarket, High Street, Castlehill and Canongate to name a few. The main three punishments were burning at the stake, hanging and the guillotine, always with large audiences in attendance.

In some instances gallows were erected on the site of the incident as in the case of the Highwaymen Thomas Kelly and Henry O'Neil two Irish immigrants who robbed a traveller David Loch on his way to Edinburgh and were sentenced to death by hanging (January 1815). Thomas Kelly and Henry O'Neil were taken to the place of execution where temporary Gibbets had been erected on the site of the robbery and they hung side by side for their crime. The site can be seen in Braid Road Edinburgh 200 metres from the corner at Morningside Station where the two Squares marked in the road and a plaque on the pavement outside 66 Braid Road Edinburgh donate where the gallows stood.

HILLEND ARTIFICIAL SKI SLOP PENTLAND HILLS

Hillend has had an artificial ski slop open to the public since the 1960s and is the largest dry slop in Europe. There are activities for all ages Skiing, Snowboarding and Tubing with floodlights on all slops for evening use and a chairlift and towlines to get you to the top. You can hire equipment and visit the lodge or take the lift to the top for a fantastic view. A great day out for the whole family especially on hot days. Which are few and far between in our wonderful Scottish climate.

HERMITAGE OF BRAID AND BLACKFORD HILL LOCAL NATURE RESERVE

GREEN WITH YELLOW NUMBERS = PAGE IN LEITH BOOK   BLUE WITH YELLOW NUMBERS = PAGE IN CITY BOOK

BLACKFORD POND

BLACKFORD POND

MAIN GATE

31 BLACKFORD POND
FEEDING THE BIRDS

28 BORE STONE

QUEEN VICTORIA PLAQUE

27

TOMMY ARMOUR
30 BIRTH PLACE

MORNINGSIDE

MAIN GATE

BLACKFORD HILL

31

42 KING'S BUILDINGS
UNIVERSITY OF EDINBURGH

31 THE ROYAL OBSERVATORY BLACKFORD HILL

30 HANGING STANES

HERMITAGE PARK

NATURE WALK

BRAID HILLS DRIVE

30   30

WESTERN GOLF CLUB

BRAID HILLS GOLF COURSE

LIBERTON TOWER 29

The Blackford Hill is a nature reserve and can provide the whole family with many interesting things to do. There is a children's play area and a pond that has many different birds (swans, geese and ducks and many more). Explore the hill and visit the Royal Observatory and see the stars in the sky. Follow the Braid Burn for some 2 miles or climb to the top (540 feet) for a great view of the city and coast. The main entrance is on Charterhall Road, you can also gain access from Observatory Road or Braid Road. Follow the Braid Burn through to the Hermitage at Morningside where it is a short walk to the Braid Hills, where the Braid Golf Course is situated. The Braid golf course is where the professional golfer Thomas Armour played as a boy before immigrating to America.

SHEEP HEID INN The Causway, Duddingston Village known originally as Dodin Village. It is said that a drinking house has been on the site since the 1300s and Bonnie Prince Charlie may have drank here before the Battle of Prestonpans in 1745. There is no definite proof of how old the pub is or how it got its name but Royalty played skittles in the back yard and a bowling alley was built in 1870. A club founded in 1882 still exists and plays once a week. A gift given to the landlord in 1580 by King James VI was a rams head snuff box, which is now in Dalmeny House and a copy is behind the bar. The village was known for the slaughter of sheep and the use of the heads for soup (powsowadie) a local broth.

THE NIGHT BEFORE THE BEGINNING OF THE END

Camped around Dunsapie Loch on Arthur Seat the army of Bonnie Prince Charlie awaited instructions from the war council being held in the house pictured below in Duddingston Village on the night of the 19 September 1745 before the Battle of Prestonpans took place. The Battle at Prestonpans was an monumental victory for the Jacobite army over the English army of red coats. The Jacobite army lead by Bonnie Prince Charlie (Charles Edward Stuart) went on to battle their way as far as Derby, before turning back with the might of the English army in chase. After 7 months of battles, the end came in just 20 minutes at the battle of Culloden where the English wiped out the Jacobites and ended the Stuarts regaining the throne, Bonnie Prince Charlie fled to Skye and then into Europe.

LOUPIN-ON-STANE

Duddingston Village has been settled since the 12th century. Once a busy weaving centre, it produced a coarse linen cloth known as 'Duddingston hardings'. Ancient cultivation terraces can still be seen behind the village below Arthur's Seat, and late Bronze Age artefacts were found in the loch in 1778.

Duddingston Kirk dates from the 12th century. The fine romanesque doorway and chancel arch still remain, and outside the gate there is a 17th century 'loupin-on-stane' to help horsemen mount, and the 'jougs', a punishment collar.

Duddingston Manse was once the home of the landscape painter, the Reverend John Thomson, Minister from 1805-1840. Famous visitors included J. M. W. Turner and Sir Walter Scott, an elder of the Kirk, who wrote part of 'Heart of Midlothian' in the Manse garden.

Prince Charlie's Cottage in The Causeway is a restored early 18th century building. Here Prince Charles Edward Stuart held his Council of War before the Battle of Prestonpans in 1745.

The Sheep Heid Inn is said to be one of the oldest in Scotland. An inn has stood on this site since the 16th century. In 1580 King James VI presented the landlord with an embellished ram's head. The present building is mainly 19th century, with an old bowed stair and skittle alley behind.

Duddingston Loch was the ice-rink of the famous Duddingston Curling Society. Since 1925 it has been a bird sanctuary.

WHERE THE WAR COUNCIL WAS HELD

BONNIE PRINCE CHARLIE

JOUGS

CRAIGMILLAR CASTLE EDINBURGH

Craigmillar Castle is one of the best-preserved medieval castles in Scotland. It has a central tower house which is surrounded by a courtyard wall and has a chapel and a do'cot. Craigmillar Castle was built in the late 14th century by the Preston family, Land owners of Craigmillar. Craigmillar Castle is best known for its association with Mary Queen of Scots. She used the castle as a place to rest after illness and after the birth of her son the future James I of England. Mary arrived at Craigmillar Castle on the 20th November 1566 and left on 7 December 1566. In November Bothwell met with nobles at Craigmillar Castle to discuss Lord Darnley. They came up with two options, divorce or assassination. They then consulted with Mary, she ruled out divorce, because it would make her son illegitimate. As for 'other means', she said that she wanted 'nothing against her honour'. The nobles saw this as her agreement to kill her husband and on leaving the nobles signed an agreement to murder Darnley. A pact known as the "Craigmillar Bond" was made, to be rid of her husband Lord Darnley. The garden pond shaped as the initial "P" can still be seen.

It was Simon Prestons' town House in Edinburgh that Mary Queen of Scots spent her last night before she was taken to Leven then on to England to spend the next 19 years in imprisonment before her execution. It was Elizabeth I the cousin of Mary Queen of Scots that had her executed.

HISTORIC TRIVIA

JAMES TYTLER. 1745 – 1804 James Tytler was the first to pilot a hot air balloon in Britain 27 August 1874. After a number of attempts he finally floated almost 1/2 a mile which has confirmed his place in the history of flight. The journey began at an area close to the foot of Arthur Seat. There are streets now named after him. The world's first man balloon flight was the Montgolfier brothers in France in 1783.

HENRY SINCLAIR 1345 – 1404 Baron of Roslin, Earl of Orkney, Lord of Shetland Sailed from Orkney to Nova Scotia in 1398 prior to Christopher Columbus discovering the West Indies. Did he discover the Americas?

NORTH BRITISH DISTILLERY Edinburgh's only surviving Whisky distillery opened in 1885 in Gorgie on the west side of Edinburgh and is still in production. Originally founded by Andrew Usher, William Sanderson and John Crabbie.

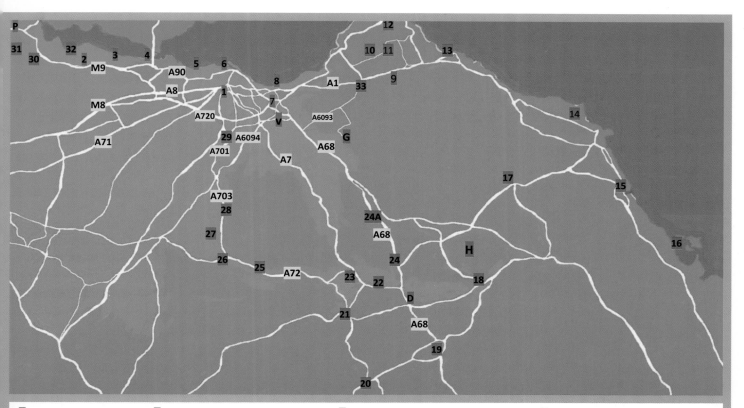

1	EDINBURGH CITY	**2**	LINLITHGOW PALACE	**3**	HOPETOUN HOUSE	**4**	SOUTH QUEENSFERRY
5	CRAMOND	**6**	LEITH SHORE	**7**	CARBERRY / FA'SIDE CASTLE	**8**	PRESTONPANS
9	HAILES CASTLE	**10**	ATHELSTANEFORD	**11**	MUSEUM OF FLIGHT	**12**	NORTH BERWICK
13	DUNBAR	**14**	COLDINGHAME / ST ABBS	**15**	BERWICK UPON TWEED	**16**	HOLY ISLAND
17	DUNS	**18**	KELSO	**19**	JEDBURGH	**20**	HAWICK
21	SELKIRK	**22**	MELROSE	**23**	GALASHIELS	**24**	EARLSTON **24A** LAUDER
25	INNERLEITHEN	**26**	PEEBLES	**27**	CRINGLETIE HOUSE	**28**	EDDLESTON
29	ROSSLYN CHAPEL	**30**	THE KELPIES	**31**	FALKIRK WHEEL	**32**	BO'NESS STEAM TRAIN
33	HADDINGTON	**D**	DRYBURGH ABBEY	**P**	DUNMORE PINEAPPLE	**V**	VOGRIE COUNTRY PARK
G	GLENKINCHIE DISTILLERY	**A68** Yellow with black number is road I.D.				**22** Red with black number places to see	

The above are just a few places to visit just outside Edinburgh, all have things of historic or cultural importance that are worth seeing. Visit the Abbeys at Jedburgh, Kelso, Dryburgh and Melrose, the chapel at Rosslyn and the Castles at Dirleton, Tantalon, Fa'side and Hailes. Out west is Linlithgow Palace, the steam train in Bo'ness, The Kelpies at Grangemouth (largest equine statues in the world) and The Falkirk Wheel the only barge lift in the world.

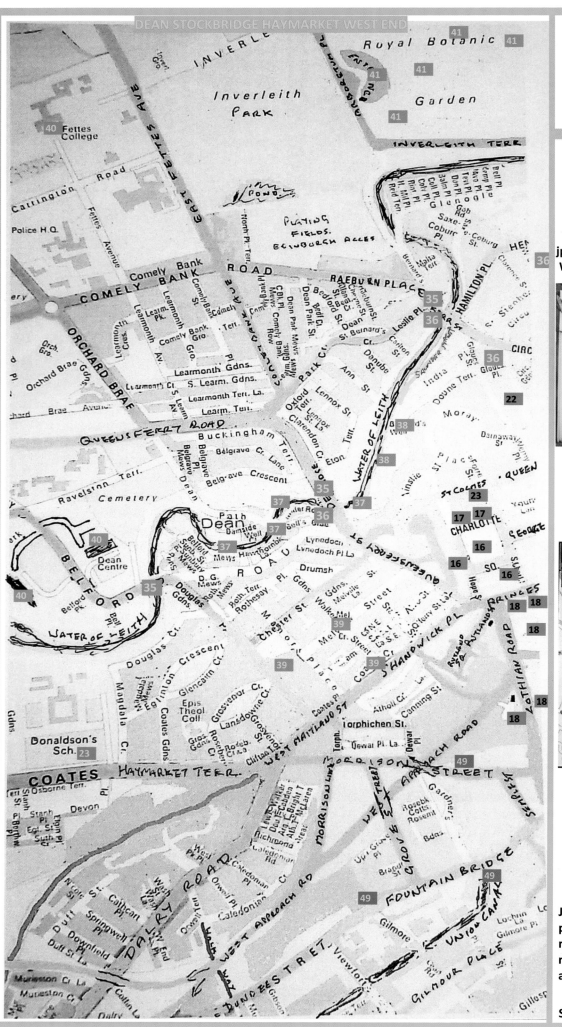

THE DEAN BRIDGE AND DEAN VILLAGE EDINBURGH

Things to be seen in the Dean area are the 2 Art Galleries, The Dean Cemetery, Dean Bridge, St Bernard's Well and St George's Well, the Water of Leith Walkway, the Royal Botanic Gardens and on a Sunday there is an outdoor market near to St Bernard's Well at Kerr Street Stockbridge.

DEAN BRIDGE

STOCKBRIDGE

THE DEAN BRIDGE EDINBURGH was designed by Thomas Telford, and was completed in 1831. The Dean Bridge was Thomas Telford's last project at the age 73 and retirement. The Dean Bridge is 447 feet long (136m) and 39 feet broad (12m) and built on four arches rising 106 feet (32m) above the river. Prior to the building of the Dean Bridge the only way across the river in to Edinburgh was by a ford in the river, which had been crossed since medieval times (5th to 15th centuries). A single-arch stone bridge near to the same spot was built for ease of crossing at the foot of Bell's Brae in the Dean Village previously of wooden construction. The river is the Water of Leith which flows from the Pentland Hills to the Port of Leith where it joins the Firth of Forth before joining the North Sea. There is a walk way at the side of the river with a visitors centre in Lanark Road that can give you detailed information on the best routes. The Water of Leith walkway extends from the Shore at Leith to Balerno a village suburb of Edinburgh over 19 km from the shore. The pathway is suitable for walking or cycling.

BELFORD BRIDGE This crossing was built to help with the heavy flow of traffic that used the Dean Bridge in the 1880s.

In the centre of the Dean village is the Bells Brae Bridge (pictured above right) the original crossing point of the Water of Leith. This stands below the Belford Bridge which was built in 1887 to carry Belford Road, part of the old road from Edinburgh to Queensferry. Dean Village was a small village outside Edinburgh and was famous as a grain milling area for over 800 years, the name Dean (Dene) meaning Deep Gorge, as you can see the village has steep hills on all sides. It is now a popular residential area with the benefits of it's proximity to the city centre.

COMMEMORATIVE STONE

Carved in the stone on the Belford Bridge is:

**ERECTED BY THE MAGISTRATES
AND TOWN COUNCIL OF THE CITY OF EDINBURGH
WITH THE AID OF THE LOCAL SUBSCRIPTIONS
OBTAINED BY THE BELFORD BRIDGE ASSOCIATION
OPENED BY
THE RT HON SIR THOMAS CLARK (BART) LORD PROVOST
JULY 1887**

HORSE RIDER EAGLE bronze was sculpted by Eoghan Bridge who was born in Edinburgh in 1963. The sculptor was completed in 1997 and can be found at the corner of a new housing development in Silvermills, Stockbridge. There is also a further statue on the bridge at Festival Square Lothian Road.

While in Edinburgh visit the Stockbridge Sunday Market 200 yards from St Bernard's Well and next to the Water of Leith. Stockbridge has many shops, bars and restaurants and is close to the city centre.

JOHN WILSON a writer, author, advocate and Professor of moral philosophy at the University of Edinburgh. He was most frequently identified by his pseudonym Christopher North.

He lived at his mother's house No 6 Gloucester Place with his family due to almost bankruptcy caused by his uncle's dishonest speculation with his money. Through hard work he recovered to move his family to their new home in Ann Street where he remained until his death in 1854. His statue stands in East Princes Street Gardens between the mound precinct and the Walter Scott monument.

TRIVIA Sir Ernest Shackleton Antarctic explorer lived at 14 South Learmonth Gardens from 1904 -1910. There are also great views of Fettes College in this area. Where ex - Prime Minister Tony Blair went to school.

DEAN BRIDGE. The Dean Bridge was designed by Thomas Telford. The Dean Bridge took 3 years to build and was opened in 1832. This was Thomas Telford's last project before he died at the age of 77.Thomas Telford was born in Eskdale Scotland.

DEAN BRIDGE The house on the corner of the bridge was once a Tavern and Bakers, the square panel on the wall shows a sun with two arms below one holding scales and the other a wheat sheaf with two baker's paddles crossed.

The inscription below reads:

**IN THE SWEAT OF THY FACE SHALT THOU
EAT BREAD GEN 3 VERSE 19
ANNO DOM 1619**

WHISKY FROM THE DEAN VILLAGE

The Water of Leith around the area of the Dean Village was the site of a number of Distilleries which are now closed. The Sunbury and Dean Distillers both closed many years ago but you can still get the taste of the Dean Whisky as it is now made at the Loch Lomond Distillery to the same traditional recipe as it was made in the Dean Distillery from 1818 to 1922.

DEAN VILLAGE

The Dean Village with the Water of Leith flowing through, grew as a community in the 1100s from the mills that were built on the river banks. The most impressive building is of Well Court, built in 1886 by the then owner of the Scotsman newspaper Sir John Findlay. The court had its own hall for socialising with a clock tower a communal court yard and a number of tenements for local workers. You will see many stones carved with crossed paddles of the bakers, as this area supplied all the bakers of Edinburgh with there flour. The old Tolbooth was a Granary built in 1675. The stone carving shows the sign of the bakers crossed paddles. At the side of the bridge is Bell's Brae House a merchant's house built in the mid-1600s. On the pathway towards Leith under the Dean Bridge is an area called Miller's Row where you can see three mill stones resting against each other previously used in the Granaries in the 1600s. 70 meters west of the bridge is a waterfall and there is a great variety of wild life. A resident near the waterfall is the Grey Heron and with luck you could spot wild otters.

WELL COURT

WATER OF LEITH AT DEAN VILLAGE

Access to Edinburgh was by a bridge, a wooden structure across the water of Leith which was rebuilt in 1801 as you see it know.

MILLER'S ROW

OLD TOLBOOTH GRANARY   BELL'S BRAE HOUSE

OLD TOLBOOTH DOOR

BELL'S BRAE BRIDGE is where the original crossing to Edinburgh was in the 5th century a single arch bridge wide enough for a carriage with horses. This was the only way across the Water of Leith and the main link on the route from Edinburgh to the Queens Ferry before the Belford Bridge and Dean Bridges were built diverting flow of traffic away from the Dean Village.

MILL STONES @ MILLER'S ROW

ST BERNARD'S WELL 1789

A natural mineral spring was discovered on the Water of Leith near to Stockbridge in 1760, some claimed that the water could cure everything. In 1789 a building was erected over the well a Doric Temple with a dome and statue inside of Hygeia the Greek goddess of health. It was called St Bernard's Well. Another well was also found a short distance west and this was called St George's Well. This was also to have the same powers as St Bernard's Well.

ST GEORGE'S WELL 1810

WATER OF LEITH AT ST BERNARDS WELL

HYGEIA GREEK GODDESS OF HEALTH

The archway to St Bernard's Well (THE DENE) on the water of Leith walkway.

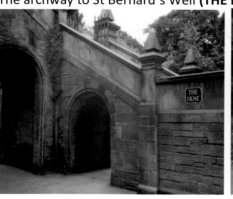

ST MARY'S EPISCOPAL CATHEDRAL PALMERSTON PLACE EDINBURGH

The actual name is The Cathedral Church of St Mary in Edinburgh. St Mary's is Scotland's Largest Cathedral and has been since 1879. St Mary's is easily spotted on Edinburgh's skyline due to being the only church with three spires. The Cathedral is dedicated to St Mary the Virgin. The highest tower is 90 meters in height and the other 2 are both 60 meters high. The Cathedral is open every day to all who wish to visit. If you continue past St Mary's Cathedral down the hill you will come to the Belford Bridge and an entrance to the water of Leith walkway, over the bridge and round the corner are the Modern Art Galleries One and Two.

GLADSTONE MEMORIAL stands in Coates Crescent of Shandwick Place at the west end of Princes Street at the tram stop. The memorial shows William Gladstone surrounded by women.

The monument was constructed in 1917 and originally stood in St Andrew Square and was moved to Coates Crescent Gardens in 1955. Gladstone was a very important public figure in Britain. Born in 1809 Gladstone served as Prime Minister for four terms, being appointed to the post on 1868, 1880, 1886, and 1892. Gladstone founded a church foundation to help women prostitutes. He was affectionately known as the 'Grand Old Man' by his many supporters and as 'God's Only Mistake' by his enemies, especially Benjamin Disraeli, the then leader of the Conservative Party.

ROBERT DUNDAS 2ND VICOUNT MELVILLE 1771 -1851

Son of Henry Dundas (1st Viscount Melville), was born in Edinburgh and educated at Gottingen University Germany and the University of Edinburgh. He was a Member of Parliament, 1st Lord of the Admiralty, and Governor of the Bank of Scotland as his father before him. Robert Dundas was awarded the Knight of the Thistle in 1821. His home was Melville Castle where he died in 1851. Pictured below is the Dundas family crest outside the door of Melville Castle.

HEART OF MIDLOTHIAN MEMORIAL CLOCK

The clock is in honoured memory of the players and members of the Heart of Midlothian football Club who lost their lives in the world wars (unveiled in 1922).

ROBERT DUNDAS

ABOVE THE LIONS HEAD   ESSAYEZ
(KEEP TRYING)
BELOW THE SHIELD   QUOD POTUI PERFECI
(I HAVE DONE WHAT I COULD TO THE BEST OF MY ABILITY)

MODERN ART 1 / MODERN ART 2

DEAN GALLERY / MODERN ART TWO

The Dean Gallery building was designed in 1830 by Thomas Hamilton and was originally an orphanage. The Gallery opened in 1999 and is home for the Eduardo Paolozzi collection. In the grounds are sculpture and graphic art, It contains a large collection of Dada and Surrealist art and literature and also holds temporary exhibitions. There is a café for refreshments.

SCOTTISH NATIONAL GALLERY OF MODERN ART
MODERN ART ONE

The building was originally the home of John Watson's Hospital (school) built in 1828 by William Burn and closed in 1975 due to lack of funding. The gallery opened at its present address in 1984. Set in large grounds it features a stepped S-shaped landform by Charles Jenks which provides the setting for a range of sculptures. The Gallery collection has approximately 5000 pieces ranging from prints and paintings to contemporary video installations are all house in the gallery. There is a café for refreshments.

SIR WILLIAM FETTES (FETTES COLLEGE)

Sir William Fettes was born on 25 June 1750. When he was eighteen he went into business as a grocer, trading in wine and tea from Smith's Land at Bailie Fyfe's Close in the High Street Edinburgh. He retired from trading Tea and Wine in 1800 to concentrate on his many other investments. He was also twice Lord Provost of Edinburgh. William Fettes lived at 13 Charlotte Square up to 1810 when he purchased the estate of Comely Bank not far from the school's present location. In his will he made a bequest which was to lead to the foundation of Fettes College. The school itself opened in 1870, 34 years after Sir William's death and is now one of the top private schools in Edinburgh. There have been many famous students attend Fettes College none more famous than British Prime Minister Tony Blair.

ROYAL BOTANIC GARDEN   EDINBURGH

GLASS HOUSE   ROYAL BOTANIC GARDENS   WEST GATE

The Botanic Gardens have displays of plants from around the world in over 28 hectares of beautifully landscaped grounds. Britain's tallest Palm House, 100 Year old hedge over 8 metres high, rock gardens, woodland gardens and arboretum, Pringle Chinese Collection, Azalea Lawn, Alpines and the Winter garden. A variety of animals and there is also a café and restaurant.

ROCK GARDENS

THE HEDGE over 23 feet high and 100 years old.

The Royal Botanic Gardens in Edinburgh was first sited at Holyrood Park beside the Abbey in 1670. It moved to Leith Walk in 1670s where it remained before finally moving to its present location in 1820. The Gardens were the imagination of two doctors Andrew Balfour and Robert Sibbald who collected plant specimens from all over Europe when on their travels. In the early 1900s a plant hunter George Forrest introduced over 10,000 specimens and the gardens continue to grow to this day.

The Botanic Gardens are open from 10.00 am every day.

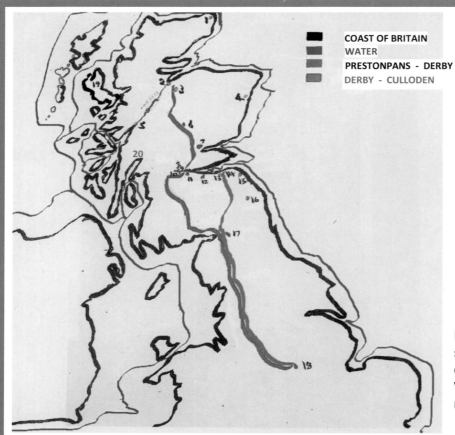

1 JOHN O GROATS
2 INVERNESS
3 BATTLE OF CULLODEN 1746
4 ABERDEEN
5 FORT WILLIAM
6 BATTLE OF KILLIECRANKIE 1689
7 PERTH
8 SIEGE OF STIRLING CASTLE 1304
9 BATTLE AT STIRLING BRIDGE 1297
10 BATTLE OF BANNOCKBURN 1596
11 BATTLE OF FALKIRK 1298
12 EDINBURGH CAPITAL OF SCOTLAND
13 BATTLE OF PINKIE CLEUGH 1547
14 BATTLE OF PRESTONPANS 1745
15 BATTLE OF DUNBAR 1296
16 BATTLE OF FLODDEN FIELD 1513
17 CARLISLE
18 DERBY
19 ISLE OF SKYE BRIDGE ON THE TRENT 1745
20 DUNADD FIRST CAPITAL OF SCOTLAND 500 AD

Legend:
- COAST OF BRITAIN
- WATER
- PRESTONPANS - DERBY
- DERBY - CULLODEN

PRESTONPANS MURAL TRAIL
Prestonpans has its history painted on its street walls. Look for the murals displayed on the walls around the town. Visitors can find the Mural trail maps next to the Totem Pole.

Map of route Bonnie Prince Charlie and the Jacobite Army marched. Prestonpans to Derby and back to Culloden. September 1745 - April 1746.

PRESTONPANS 1745 THE JACOBITE UPRISING The beginning of the end of the fight for the throne of Britain for the Young pretender Charles Edward Stuart known as Bonnie Prince Charlie. The battle for the crown began in Prestonpans on 21 September 1745 and ended in Culloden on 16 April 1746 less than 7 months and thousands of deaths with Charles escaping to France where he lived till his death. After Culloden the English troops run riot through Scotland and made the kilt illegal dress and disbanded the clans a dark time in Scottish history.

THE BATTLE FLAG The Pyramid marks the area where the Battle of Prestonpans took place in 1745. Bonnie Prince Charlie led the Jacobite Army in a triumph over the English. There is a story board at the summit of the Pyramid with the story of the Jacobite uprising and the route to glory and defeat.

THE WALLACE MONUMENT

CAMBUSKENNETH ABBEY

The Wallace Monument was completed in 1869 and stands over 500 feet (152m) above the Stirling Bridge where he had his most famous victory of the English. There is a bronze statue of William Wallace on the outside of the monument. Once you climb the short hill to the monument 246 steps await you, to get a fantastic view of the area from the crown of the monument on level 4. The monument has 4 levels and on each level there are things worth the climb to see. Level 1 Hall of Arms, level 2 Hall of Heroes, level 3 the Royal Chamber and then to the top.

Cambuskenneth Abbey was founded in 1140 by David I. King James III and his wife Margaret of Denmark are both buried in their tomb beside the Abbey.

THE GOTHENBURG in Prestonpans built in 1908 still runs under the original Gothenburg Public-house system. Where the majority of the income is given to charity to benefit the community. The system was originally started in Sweden in 1855 to control the consumption of alcohol.

THE PRESTONPANS MURALS show the history of the area and the Murals Trail starts at the Gothenburg and winds its way around the streets of Prestonpans. There are over 30 Murals to see and include John Knox, The Witches Gate, Sir Walter Scott and Tam O'Shanter . There is also a number of things to see in the Burns Memorial Garden.

There are many things to see in Prestonpans, the Prestongrange outdoor museum and Café which is across from part of the John Muir Way that follows the coast of East Lothian where seals can be seen in the shallows. A great place to cycle or walk with fantastic views of Edinburgh. With story boards that show how the Harbour once was. The many murals throughout the town showing the towns history of making soap and salt.

ARTHUR SEAT FROM PRESTONPANS

PRESTONPANS TOTEM POLES The one that stands across from the Gothenburg was carved from a red cedar tree from Chemainus Vancouver Island British Columbia, Canada. The carvings give a pictorial story of the area and was erected in 2006 when the 6th Global Murals Conference took place in Prestonpans. Halfway up you can see the number 81 in memory of the Witches that were burnt unjustly and then pardoned in 2004. The other Totem poles and the mural of the Witches Trial can be seen in the play park.

THE WITCH TRIALS

PRESTON TOWER AND GARDENS

Preston Tower is no long accessible but can be seen from the beautiful well-kept gardens. The Tower was built in an L-shape in the late 1300s or early 1400s and was the home of the Hamilton's of Preston. The area around the Tower was once called Preston. With a very unfortunate past the Tower has been burnt 3 times 1544, 1650 and again in 1663 and has been vacant since. In the far corner of the gardens is a do' cot which is still in use by the local pigeons. There is also a very impressive laburnum arch.

PRESTONPANS MERCAT CROSS

The Mercat Cross that stands in Prestonpans is the oldest remaining Mercat Cross in its original form and position in Scotland. Five Mercat Cross were built in the early 1600s all to the same design and for the same purpose, to make important civic announcements. Edinburgh's Mercat Cross is still used for government proclamations that affected all of Scotland. An example, announcements concerning successions to the monarchy and the calling to parliament. There is an entrance to steps which bring you out at a platform where the announcements are read. The Unicorn is the ancient emblem of Scotland and stands at the top of the Mercat Cross.